ICE BREAKERS

HOW TO GET ANY PROSPECT TO BEG YOU FOR A PRESENTATION

TOM "BIG AL" SCHREITER

DEDICATION

This book is dedicated to network marketers everywhere.

I travel the world 240+ days each year. Let me know if you want me to stop in your area and conduct a live Big Al training.

http://www.BigAlSeminars.com

Get 7 mini-reports of amazing, easy sentences that create new, hot prospects.

Sign up today at:
http://www.BigAlReport.com

Other great Big Al Books available at:

http://www.BigAlBooks.com

Table of Contents

PREFACE

"Success leaves clues."

Yes, that is true, but failure leaves clues also. It was 1972, early in my network marketing career. I tried to get appointments but the prospects said, "No." I tried to start conversations with potential prospects and they quickly changed the subject and looked for excuses to exit. I advertised for "hot" prospects, and they replied that they weren't interested in what I had to offer.

What was the clue that became obvious from all this failure?

All of my conversations started with the same basic phrases about my wonderful opportunity. The phrases I chose compelled my prospects to say, "No." Repeating these wrong, untrained phrases over and over again to new prospects didn't fix the problem. The problem was that I was saying the wrong words.

Unless I changed my opening words (my Ice Breakers), then nothing would change in my career. So here is a book on proven Ice Breakers so failure doesn't have to leave you that same clue.

-- Tom "Big Al" Schreiter

Ugh! Ouch! Groan!

- "Do you have a residual income Plan B?"

- "I am in an awesome business with awesome products with awesome founders with an awesome compensation plan with awesome training …"

- "Have you considered your income opportunity options?"

- "You look like a depressed full-time loser, would you like a chance to be a winner?"

- "The economy is in the toilet. Would you like to be sitting on top?"

- "Are you going to be a lowly jobholder all of your life?"

- "Do you want multiple streams of income?"

Yes, these are Ice Breakers that start a conversation, but they are really, really **bad** ones. Even if these examples didn't get us instant rejection, we certainly haven't started off on the good side of our prospect.

We all talk to people. The problem is we say the **wrong** things.

We are not afraid to talk to people. We are comfortable saying, "Hi, how are you, how is the weather?"

But there's a big gap between saying:

"Hi, how are you, how is the weather?"

and

"Want to be a distributor?"

And that big gap **scares** us. It is hard to transition from friendly social talk to introducing your business into the conversation without feeling like a pushy salesman. We need to "break the ice" and introduce our business into the conversation in a socially acceptable way.

If we don't know how to do this gracefully, we simply keep our business top secret. Then, no one knows about our business and nobody joins our business.

Now, we don't want to ruin our relationships with people. We don't want to take advantage of our relatives. But if we don't get this right, if we don't know what to say, then we will have no one to talk to.

Here's a cool secret.

The only difference between the people that have **unlimited** prospects in network marketing and those who don't ... is what they say. Knowing the exact words to say is the skill everyone needs to introduce your business into the conversation.

You see, we already have a good attitude. We went to the opportunity meeting. We already believe in our company. We have goals. We know what we want. We're motivated. We're positive. We have all these things.

The only things we don't have are the skills of exactly **what to say** and exactly **what to do**. The good news is that we can learn them.

Many distributors have the same compensation plan, the same territory, the same products, and the same pricing. All of the circumstances are the same in their career except one thing:

"What they say and do."

"What they say and do," not their circumstances, will determine the size of their bonus checks.

So it is time to learn to say better stuff. Let's begin.

Why I Suffer While You Are Rich And Happy.

Let's say that we're both distributors. After the regular weekly opportunity meeting, I go to Denny's Restaurant to get a late-night meal. I sit at a table and the waitress comes up and says,

"What would you like to order?"

I reply, "Oh, I'd like to order a hamburger, French fries, a side salad, a Caesar salad, some macaroni and cheese, garlic bread, a blueberry muffin, apple pie, ice cream, some chocolate cake and a Diet Coke."

The waitress brings the food. I eat. I leave to go to my car in the parking lot and I say to myself,

"What a poor and miserable business. Nobody here is interested in opportunity. Nobody wants a part-time job. Nobody wants to invest money to start a business. Nobody wants to be a salesman. Everyone just wants to watch television when they go home. What a poor and miserable business!"

Now you attend the same weekly opportunity meeting. After the meeting, you go to Denny's Restaurant also to get your late-night meal. You sit at the table next to me, and the same waitress comes up to you and says,

"What would you like to order?"

And you say, "Are you married to your job or are you open-minded?"

The waitress thinks for a second and says, "What?"

You repeat, "Are you married to your job or are you open-minded?"

The waitress quickly says, "Hey, I'm open-minded. I don't want to be a waitress at Denny's Restaurant all my life. What's it all about?"

You reply, "Well. I can't talk to you now. You're at work."

The waitress interrupts,

"Well, do you have a brochure? Can you send me to a website? What is your telephone number? Do you have a business card? Do you have a CD or a DVD? What's it all about? I have a coffee break coming up in 30 minutes, I can follow you out to your car. When can we talk?"

You finish your meal at Denny's Restaurant and go to your car and think,

"What a poor and miserable business. I can't even have a meal at Denny's without people harassing me, asking for opportunity, asking for presentations. I have to push prospects away just to finish my meal!"

Whoa, what was the difference?

We both went to Denny's Restaurant to eat. We both had the same waitress. The only difference is that **you chose different words.**

Because you chose different "trained words," you have unlimited prospects begging you for a presentation and are living the life of your dreams. Because I chose "untrained words," I complain that no one wants to do my business and I spend my network marketing career in frustration.

The only difference in this scenario is that you **chose different words.** Everything else was the same.

These few words ("Are you married to your job or are you open-minded?") separate me, with my life of frustration and no bonus checks, from you, enjoying unlimited pre-sold prospects and the life of your dreams.

Just a few trained words.

Prospects Are Everywhere, If You Know What To Say.

Later that day I need a battery for my camera. I stop by the local electronics store and I pick up a single AAA battery. I walk up to the cashier and I say,

"I would like to purchase this AAA battery."

The cashier replies, "That will be $1.00. Do you want a warranty with that?"

Bravely I say, "No, no, no, I'll risk the whole dollar."

I walk out into the parking lot and grumble:

"What a poor and miserable business. Nobody wants opportunity in this city. Nobody wants more income in their life. Everybody's happy with their job. Nobody's a salesman. Everybody believes it's a pyramid. What a poor and miserable business."

You stand right behind me in line at the cash register at the electronics store. After I finish the purchase of my battery and walk out of the store, you come up to the same cashier and say,

"I would like to purchase this AAA battery."

The cashier says, "That will be $1.00. Do you want a warranty with that?"

And you say, "No, I'll risk it. But I'm curious, have you found a chance to be your own boss so that you don't have to work 40 hours a week?"

The cashier thinks for a moment and says, "What?"

You repeat, "Have you found a chance to be your own boss already, so that you don't have to work 40 hours a week for the rest of your life?"

The cashier smiles, "No, of course not, that's why I'm working here for minimum wage."

And then you say,

"Well, I know you are busy and don't have much time to look, but when you decide to start looking, here is my card. Just give me a call."

And as you're walking out the cashier says, "Hey, I don't have to give you a call, I'm looking. What's it all about?"

You reply, "Well, you're at work, I can't talk to you now."

The cashier panics.

"Oh no, well, here's my home number. I get home tomorrow at 5:00 pm, give me a call at home. If you can't reach me at home, call me on my cell phone. If you miss me, leave a message on voicemail. I'll get right back to you. Is there a brochure I can look at, a website I can go to? Please tell me a little bit about it."

As you walk into the parking lot you say,

"What a poor and miserable business. I can't even pick up a battery without being constantly harassed. People begging for opportunity. Looking for presentations."

What was the difference?

You go shopping and have prospects begging you for a presentation. I shop at the same places you do, see the same people you do, but have no prospects.

The difference?

You and I chose **different words** when we were in contact with the same people.

If we get Ice Breakers right, we have lots of prospects and a thriving business. If we use "untrained words" when we meet people, it's going to be a poor and miserable business.

Everywhere I Travel In The World, This Problem Occurs.

The new distributor comes to me and says:

"I just need to be a better closer."

I reply, "Great, great, great. Well, learn to be a better closer. But I am just curious, how many presentations do you give every week?"

The new distributor says, "Oh, about none."

I say, "Maybe closing isn't your problem. Let's talk about presentations. How many appointments do you have for presentations every week?"

The new distributor says, "Oh, about none."

I continue, "Maybe giving presentations isn't your problem. How many people do you ask or ask you for an appointment every week?"

The new distributor says, "Oh, about none."

There is the problem.

Most new distributors spend all of their week **looking** for someone to give a presentation to!

So instead of spending the entire week looking for someone to give a presentation to, wouldn't it make more sense to learn the Ice Breaker skills so that you could spend the entire week **giving** presentations?

How would that change your career?

Well, first of all, you wouldn't be stressed and always looking for prospects.

Second, if you had lots of presentations to give that week, your positioning with prospects would be powerful. You wouldn't worry if one person joined or not, since you had a full week of presentations to get to. Prospects can smell desperation when you don't have prospects.

Third, with good Ice Breaker skills you could get all of your new distributors off to a great start.

Don't Fall For These Myths.

We have to think clearly, because this is a business. We can't run a business on myths and old wives' tales.

Myth: But I have to find special people!

No. You don't have to find special people. Almost everyone you talk to is ... **pre-sold!** How awesome is that?

Think about it. When you talk to prospects, do they want more money in their lives ... or less money?

More!

They are pre-sold on finding an opportunity, but they may not be pre-sold on the words we chose to "break the ice" in our conversation.

So you may have heard more myths like these. Don't fall for them!

Myth: You can't say the wrong thing to the right person.

Of course you can say the wrong thing. That's why that person tells us "No!" instead of asking us for a presentation. Early in my career I said the wrong thing to lots of great prospects.

Myth: You can't say the right thing to the wrong person.

Really? Then how does that person eventually change? This person isn't doomed for life. Someone will finally say something that will change that person's life.

Myth: Just go out and get 100 "No" answers from prospects.

Ouch. Let me see. If 3 "No" answers hurt, why would you want 97 more "No" answers that hurt? Wouldn't it make more sense to learn "trained words" so that prospects would say "Yes" instead?

Myth: Every "No" just gets you closer to a "Yes!"

No, every "No" answer just gets you closer to another "No" answer because you are saying the wrong words. If the words you say create "No" answers, saying them more often won't change the results. Change the words if you want a different answer.

Wrong "untrained words" make people upset. When I first got started, I talked to all my relatives. And I was banned from weddings and funerals. I talked to my co-workers, and they would skip coffee breaks to avoid me. I talked to my friends, and they would walk on the other side of the street.

See a trend?

But, after I changed what I said, many of these very same people joined and became good leaders. The very same people.

It's not really finding the right person, it's saying the right "trained words." We start in network marketing, we find the right people, but we ruin them with the wrong words.

Here's a story I tell new distributors to help them remember it is not finding the right prospect, but saying the right words.

Getting a date.

Imagine that I'm single and I go to a party to meet some ladies in the hopes of getting a date. I say to the ladies I meet:

"So how old are you?"

"How much do you weigh?"

"What color do you dye your hair?"

"Are those your real teeth?"

"How much makeup do you need every morning?"

"Oh, so you are not pregnant?"

Let me ask you, how many dates am I going to get? None. Zero. I leave the party and say, "There are no good prospects at this party. Some of those ladies didn't even like men. Please, someone help me find a new party where I can find some **good** prospects!"

Well, what is going to happen at the next party? The exact same result because I say the exact same "untrained words."

But is it possible that someone else could go to that first party and get a date? Sure. That person simply would say different words.

Still unsure that words make the difference?

There are always at least two ways of describing everything. The set of words you choose will greatly affect your results. Here is an example of a young man talking to his date:

Word Choice #1. "When I look in your eyes, time stands still."

Word Choice #2. "Your face would stop a clock!"

Both sets of words roughly describe the same event, but the results would be vastly different!

Ice Breakers are the first words in a conversation where we introduce our product or opportunity. The words we choose for our Ice Breakers could mean the difference between a fantastic network marketing business, and failure.

Those First Nervous Words
To Your Sister.

Let's take a look at what happens when we start our networking career. On Sunday I go over to my sister's house for dinner. As a brand-new distributor, I am anxious to talk to my sister about my wonderful business.

So I'm eating away … munch, munch, munch, munch, munch. I've talked to her about the children. Munch, munch, munch, munch, munch. I've talked about the weather. Munch, munch, munch, munch, munch. I've talked about the local politics. Munch, munch, munch, munch, munch. I've talked about her job. Munch, munch, munch, munch, munch. I've asked her 20 questions about her life. Munch, munch, munch, munch, munch.

And at no time has my sister turned to me and said,

"Hey Bro, have you joined any new businesses lately that you would like to tell me about?"

So it is going to be up to me to "break the ice" and introduce my business into this family conversation.

Now here's the situation. Everyone can talk to other people. Anyone can say, "Hi, how are you? How's the weather?" That's easy.

But there's a huge gap between "Hi, how are you, how is the weather?" to "Want to be a distributor?"

It's that huge gap that scares us. We don't want to look like a sleazy salesperson or look like we are trying to take advantage of people. And because of that fear, we often say nothing. That kills our career.

So with my career at stake, I know I have to say something.

1. If I say something good, my sister will ask for a presentation. That would be nice.

2. But if I say something bad, what is she going to say?

"Sit on the other side of the table."

"Talk to my hand."

"Never come back for dinner here again."

And because this might get ugly, I am really, really nervous.

I keep eating away, munch, munch, munch, munch, munch. I talk more about politics, kids, her holiday, the relatives, and more about the weather! If I don't "break the ice" about my business soon, dessert will be over and it will be time to go home.

This moment … is my career.

Reality.

If I get this right, I will have lots of people to talk to. They'll ask me for presentations. If I get it wrong, I am going to starve.

So I think: "This is it. Be brave. Go for it. Visualize your goals. Car payment is due."

I take a deep breath and say, "Hey, Sis. Want to be a distributor?"

Just kidding. I would never say something stupid like that more than once or twice. Instead, I say:

"Hey, Sis. I'm in the global search for entrepreneurial talents who are looking for time freedom and financial freedom, whereby they can enhance their efforts through multiple streams of residual income, thereby leveraging and compounding their time asset ..."

I'm dead.

My sister's salesman alarm is ringing in her head. And she knows that I don't normally talk like that. Maybe some space alien has taken over my body. Plus, I am using too many industry words such as distributor, upline, downline, crossline, clothesline, BV, PV, etc.

It's going to be ugly here.

But I'm not a quitter! I try again by saying, "Hey Sis, let me tell you about the financial corporate insecurity in the world today. Financial institutions are in trouble. The World Trade Organization is keeping us in poverty. Pension plans are not guaranteed. People are losing their jobs. Both husband and wife have to work. It is the breakup of the American family. Sixty-five percent of the people are dead or should be dead ..."

I wonder if there is such a word as "dead-er"... this is going badly.

Now I'm desperate. Time to be direct. Just tell my sister about my great company and my great products. Nothing else has worked. So I say:

"Hey Sis, I'm a distributor for the Wonderful Company from the wonderful city of Wonderful, Texas, started by Mr. Wonderful himself. He is a wonderful family man. He has several wonderful families to prove it. The company has wonderful fax machines, wonderful computers, wonderful printers and everything is wonderful, wonderful, wonderful!"

What is my sister thinking? She is thinking, "Wonderful. My brother has joined a cult. And if I join, I will sound just as stupid as he does right now."

Now, there is nothing wrong with the Wonderful Company and its products. It's just that I am introducing the company at the wrong time. I need to "break the ice" first.

This is my career at this moment. And I have blown it!

Time to get serious and learn how to do Ice Breakers professionally.

The rules.

I have some rules about presentations and Ice Breakers.

Rule #1: I only give a presentation to people that **ask** me for a presentation **first**.

The reason I do this, is that I'm a full-time coward. I hate rejection. I don't want to force myself or my business on anyone.

Now I know what you are thinking:

"If I only give presentations to people who beg me for a presentation first, then I am going to starve!"

Relax. All we are going to do is learn the skill of how to get prospects to beg. For most distributors, if a prospect **asks** for a presentation, things get a lot easier.

By the way, how would your life change if all week long, people were asking you for a presentation? Life would be good, wouldn't it? So just this one little skill, Ice Breakers, could get your career moving forward fast.

Because if you have people always asking you for presentations, you're going to build some sort of business, aren't you? Even if you can't give a decent presentation, some prospects will join just out of sympathy!

Rule #2: Ice Breakers should be 100 percent rejection-free. If there is any chance of rejection, distributors will be afraid to use them.

Rule #3: Ice Breakers should never high-pressure or embarrass our sister or anybody else. If you high-pressure or embarrass your sister, you'll never be invited back for dinner, and that's a bad thing. Plus it's good manners to be polite.

Rule #4: Ice Breakers should have a high probability of success. Because if your Ice Breakers don't work, well, no one will continue to use them. We have to live with others for the rest of our life.

Formula #1.

You can create lots of great Ice Breakers with formulas. Let's use one of these formulas now.

Let's go back to my sister's house. Munch, munch, munch, munch, munch. I've talked about the weather. I've talked about everything, so I turn to my sister and say,

"Hey Sis, I just found out how we can get an extra paycheck every month. If you would ever like to know how, I would be glad to tell you. Meanwhile, please pass the peas."

Now, if my sister was interested, what might she say?

"Tell me more."

She's asking for a presentation, with no rejection!

I would say, "Sure, I'll tell you after dinner."

My sister replies, "No, no, no! Tell me more now. I need an extra paycheck."

I reply, "I will tell you after dessert, after we have cleared off the table."

My sister says, "No, tell me now!"

Is that a good problem? Yes! My sister is begging me for a presentation, rejection-free.

Now if my sister was not interested, what might she do? She would simply pass the peas and I still win because I get food! But, more importantly, there was no rejection.

Did I high-pressure or embarrass my sister in any way? No. Did this approach have a good probability of success? Yes.

So why did this work?

First, the phrase "I just found out ..." freezes the prospect's brain, brings the conscious mind to a complete halt, makes the mind forget everything it was thinking about, and compels the listener to totally focus on the words I say next. Cool, eh?

The subconscious mind has programs that run our lives. One program is "survival." So when we hear the words, "I just found out," this survival program says to us, "Stop everything. This might be important for our survival. Shhhhhh. Be quiet. Listen."

Another program is "curiosity." The curiosity program says, "**What** did you find out? I need to know what you found out. I cannot go on in life until I know what you found out. Shhhhh. Be quiet. Listen."

The prospect has no chance. The prospect has to listen. Think about it this way. If nobody is listening, your chances are pretty dim. We have to freeze the brain and get the prospect's attention.

Then, after "I just found out ..." we can insert a benefit. Now the prospect is listening closely to the benefit, and usually wants to know more about getting that benefit. So the prospect naturally asks to know more. What a great way to get prospects to ask for presentations.

What about the remainder of the Ice Breaker I used?

"If you would ever like to know how, I would be glad to tell you. Meanwhile, please pass the peas."

This gives the prospect an easy way to indicate, "No, I am not interested," by allowing them to simply pass the peas and nothing more has to be said. The prospect doesn't have to think up silly objections and excuses if he or she is not interested.

If you don't believe this works, you can test this on your own. Prove to yourself that you can freeze minds with just these four words, "I just found out …"

Try this. Do you have some relatives you would like to get even with? At the next family gathering, sit at the end of the table. Eat away. Munch, munch, munch, munch, munch. Turn to one of your relatives and say something like this, "You know, I just found out …" Never say another word. It will drive that person crazy.

Did you notice that this is simply a formula that gets prospects interested and asking for a presentation, and that it doesn't require a super attitude, a vision board, charisma or courage?

Yes, anyone can use Ice Breakers, even the shy, brand-new distributor.

So memorize Formula #1:

"I just found out" + benefit = Great Ice Breaker

And if that formula is hard to visualize, then simply fill in the blanks in this sentence:

Hey _____ ,

I just found out how to _____ .

If you would ever like to know how, I would be glad to tell you, meanwhile please _____!

Let's Have A Little Fun With This Formula.

We'll insert some benefits and see how it sounds.

You are at work and you want to talk to one of your co-workers about your business. You say to your co-worker:

"Hey Joe, I just found out how we can fire the boss, and start our own business. If you would ever like to know how, I'd be glad to tell you. Meanwhile, let's go on coffee break."

What is Joe going to say?

"Let's go on a long coffee break."

Easy, wasn't it? You know this is going to work on most people at work except ... the boss. They all will want to have a conversation with you during coffee break.

But maybe you don't go to work. Maybe you are a stay-at-home mom and your prospects are other stay-at-home moms. You could say this:

"Hey Mary, I just found out how we can stay home with our children and still get a full-time paycheck. If you'd ever like to know how, I'd be glad to tell you. Meanwhile, let's take the children to the park."

What do you think most Marys are going to say?

"Tell me more."

I've never had a Mary say, "Oh, I'd rather warehouse the children in daycare."

Do you know someone who is 50 years old? You can say:

"Hey Joe, I just found out how you can retire five years early at full pay. If you'd ever like to know how, I'd be glad to tell you. Meanwhile, let's go back to work."

Is Joe going to let you go back to work? No. He says,

"Stay right here, tell me now."

Now, that won't work for someone who is 18 years old. For him you might say:

"Hey Joe, I just found out how we don't have to work 45 years like our parents. If you would ever like to know how, I would be glad to tell you. Meanwhile, go back to playing video games."

Do you watch television with a friend? You might say something like this,

"Hey Mary, I just found out how we can work three weeks out of the month but get paid for four. If you'd ever like to know how, I'd be glad to tell you. Meanwhile let's watch the news."

Or you can say it a different way if you'd like. You could say,

"Hey Mary, I just found out how we can take a one-week holiday every month, and we don't even have to stay with our in-laws. If you'd ever like to know how, I'd be glad to tell you. Meanwhile, give me the remote control."

What do you think Mary is going to say?

"A one-week holiday with the family once a month? Yeah, we never see each other. Great idea. Tell me more."

Want to go after leaders? You're watching TV and you say,

"Hey Mary, I just found out how we can take a six-month holiday twice a year."

Yes, Mary will laugh, but then she will say, "Tell me more!"

If you talked to commuters, you could say, "Hey Joe, I just found out how we never have to waste time commuting again. If you would ever like to know how, I would be glad to tell you. Meanwhile, I hope we can get a seat on the train."

If you talked to secretaries, you could say this,

"Hey Mary, I just found out how secretaries can earn more money part-time than their bosses do full-time. If you ever want to know how, I would be glad to tell you. Meanwhile, go back to filing your nails."

Okay, that's a bit exaggerated, but this is a good template for lots of scenarios, such as:

* I just found out how housewives can earn more money part-time than their husbands do full-time.

* I just found out how government clerks can earn more money part-time than the mayor does full-time.

Use your imagination!

It is what we say that makes a difference. I hear a lot of networkers complain about university students. They say,

"What a bunch of lazy, useless, unmotivated job-seeking..."

Oh wait. Maybe it's not the university students who are at fault. Maybe it's what we said and what we did. Would you agree with me that if we said something better and did something better, at least some of them would ask us for a presentation? Maybe not all, but at least more would.

So to a university student I would say this,

"Hey Joe, I just found out how university students can earn more money part-time then their professors do full-time. If you'd ever like to know how, I'd be glad to tell you. Meanwhile, go back to playing video games and drinking beer."

I think we certainly would get more university students to ask you for a presentation by this simple change in what we say.

To a friend you could say,

"I just found out how we would never have to go to work again. If you would ever like to know how, I would be glad to tell you. Meanwhile, let's go bowling."

Or try this,

"I just found out how we can take a five-day weekend instead of a two-day weekend. If you would ever like to know how, I would be glad to tell you. Meanwhile, how is your dog?"

Or,

"I just found out how you never have to work weekends again. If you would ever like to know how, I would be glad to tell you. Meanwhile, did you see that great show on television last night?"

Let's say that the tax advantage of your business is worth $200 each month. So you are at a party, and there are three people standing around you, all holding their drinks. One turns to you and says, "So what's new with you?" And you reply,

"I just found out how we can get a $200.00 tax refund every month. If you'd ever like to know how, I'd be glad to tell you. Meanwhile, let's grab some snacks."

Are they going to let you grab snacks? No, they're going to say,

"Hey if you get it, I deserve it too. How do we get it? What do we have to do? What's it all about?"

The hardest part of network marketing is now over. They are asking you for a presentation. At this point you have the following options.

#1. Give them a CD.

#2. Give them a brochure.

#3. Send them to a website.

#4. Panic and say that you know nothing, but you will have your sponsor call them.

#5. Invite them to an opportunity meeting.

#6. Give them a sample of your company's product.

#7. Set an appointment to talk to them tomorrow.

#8. Ask them if they could be on a three-way call with your sponsor.

#9. Set an appointment to do a two-on-one presentation with them and your sponsor over coffee.

And if you had better skills, you could:

#10. Do a "One-Minute Presentation."

#11. Do a "Two-Minute Story" to their subconscious minds.

And if you had superior skills, you could do more, but the point is, you have plenty of options to choose from, even if you are brand-new to network marketing. Remember, the hardest part is over. They are asking you for a presentation.

See a pattern yet?

It is easy. The formula is:

"I just found out …" plus a benefit.

But you might be thinking, "Hey, wait a minute, these Ice Breakers are all about the opportunity. I want to talk about my product and services."

Okay, let's do some random products and service examples. We are going to say, "I just found out ..." and then add the following benefits. Ready?

For nutrition:

* How we can wake up an hour earlier every morning, feeling like a million dollars.

* How we can fall asleep within seven minutes of our head touching the pillow.

* How we can feel like we're 16 years old all over again, but with better judgment.

* How we can have more energy than our grandchildren.

* How we can have a killer immune system so nothing will "take us out."

* How we can protect our children from all the germs at school.

* How we can have enough energy to come home from work and feel like dancing.

* How we can have so much energy it would take a tranquilizer dart just to make us sit down.

* How we can get fruit and veggie nutrition into our children without them knowing it.

For skin care:

* How we can make our skin look 20 years younger in only 45 seconds a day.

* How we can put off wrinkles an extra 20 years.

* How we can make our skin younger while we sleep.

* How we can make our skin look so young, we won't be able to order alcohol at restaurants. (Okay, slightly exaggerated, but fun.)

* How we can improve our daughter's acne in just nine days.

* How we can protect our skin from the harsh winters here.

For diet products:

* How we can lose five pounds in the next 10 days.

* How we never have to go on a diet again.

* How we can lose weight easily by having this special drink for breakfast.

* How we never have to feel hungry again.

* How we can lose weight one time, and keep it off forever.

* How we can turn our body into a fat-burning machine.

* How we can lose weight while we sleep.

* How we can lose weight quickly without worrying about going on a diet.

* How we can lose weight, and we don't even have to go to the gym.

For travel:

* How we can take a five-star holiday for the price of a simple hotel room.

* How we can travel wholesale instead of retail.

* How we can see the world first-hand instead of only in pictures.

* How we can take holidays that make our neighbors jealous.

* How we can take a one-week luxury holiday every three months.

* How we can build family memories with a holiday of a lifetime.

For natural cleaning products:

* How we can clean our home without toxic chemicals.

* How we can replace poisonous cleaners with natural cleaners, and never have to worry when small children visit our home.

* How we can use natural cleaners and protect our environment.

* How we can do something good for our planet, and it is easy.

* How we don't have to put padlocks on our cleaning supplies.

For financial services:

* How we can have our savings pay for our insurance.

* How we can retire early without having to get a raise.

* How we can save for retirement by letting the government pay for it.

* How we can have more spendable income by simply changing how we pay our bills.

* How we can get out of debt quickly with one simple change.

For pets:

* How we can get our pets to outlive us.

* How we can make our pets feel young again.

* How we can give our pets the best nutrition available.

This is getting easier and easier. To get people to beg you for a presentation isn't so hard after all. We just need to master the skill of using Ice Breaker #1, and we can fill our week with giving presentations.

Does This Work On Cold Prospects?

Let's see.

If you have already built rapport with your prospect, then your Ice Breaker will sound natural and non-threatening. Building rapport should take only a couple of seconds.

If you haven't already learned the skill on how to build rapport in seconds, then I recommend reading this excellent book by my favorite author … me.

Read "How To Get Instant Trust, Belief, Influence and Rapport! 13 Ways To Create Open Minds By Talking To The Subconscious Mind."

You can find this book at http://www.BigAlBooks.com

So let's say you have established rapport in the first couple of seconds. What are you going to say to that total stranger? Here is a great example.

The desk clerk.

After your evening hotel opportunity meeting, you might stop and chat with the night desk clerk. After building rapport you could say:

"I just found out how you would never have to work evenings again. If you would ever like to know how, I would be glad to tell you. Meanwhile, where are the restrooms?"

And if the night clerk had a sense of humor, you could say:

"Hey, I just found out how you can get a full-time check and you never have to work evenings again. If you would ever like to know how, I'll be glad to tell you. Meanwhile, enjoy working until what … 5:00 am in the morning?"

Now it would be up to the night desk clerk to decide if he wanted to work evenings or if he wanted a new opportunity. If the time is right, we know he will ask for more information, for a presentation.

Are you starting to believe that Ice Breakers are all about what we say? And are you starting to believe that we need trained words?

Now, I have nothing against having a great attitude, a vision board, chanting affirmations, singing the company song, jumping higher at conventions, etc. That's all very nice.

But even if you could levitate right to the prospect with your incredible personal motivational skill, **you will still have to say something.** And it is the words you choose to say that will make the difference.

At the fuel station.

If I am in a different city at night, I can stop to fuel my car. Now, in your area, do you pay outside at the pump, or do you pay inside to the clerk?

Let me make a recommendation. Very few gas pumps actually join your business. Your prospect is inside.

After pumping my fuel, I go inside. What do I know about the clerk behind the counter?

* Is this person overpaid or underpaid?

* Does he love his job or hate his job?

* Does he like working nights and guarding somebody else's money?

* Does he enjoy his role as human target practice for criminals?

* Does he want more money and opportunity in his life?

This sounds like a prospect, doesn't it? So I just simply walk in to pay and I say something like this:

"Hey, I just found out how we can get a $200 tax refund every month. If you'd ever like to know how, I would be glad to tell you. Meanwhile, here's my credit card."

How hard was that? If he's not interested, he processes the credit card. If he's interested, he asks for more information and a presentation.

Or I could go inside to pay and say this,

"Hey, I just found out how we can get an extra paycheck so we don't have to work so hard. If you'd ever like to know how, I would be glad to tell you. Meanwhile, add on this diet soda and 44 bars of chocolate."

Some of you are thinking. "I will stop by 30 gas stations on the way home and purchase $1 worth of gas at each station. That will give me 30 new prospects to talk to."

Well, I am sure the clerk will notice you if you only buy $1 worth of gasoline, but it may not be the image or positioning we want when talking to prospects. ☺

But don't limit your thinking. You can still stop at 30 gas stations and just ask for directions to your home.

How about the waitress?

If you don't stop to fuel your car, you can stop for a cup of coffee, right? Simply talk to the waitress, build rapport, and then say,

"I just found out how you can get a full-time paycheck and don't have to wait tables in the evenings. If you'd ever like to know how, I would be glad to tell you. Meanwhile, I'd like some extra sugar for my coffee."

Simple as that.

Many distributors ask this question though, "But I have been in my business for six months already. How can I say I just found out something?"

Good question. Three quick solutions.

#1. You can say, "I found out." But it's a little weak and wimpy compared to "I just found out" which freezes people's minds and forces them to listen.

#2. I bet there's something new in your business that you just found out. Maybe a new trip incentive, a new use for your product, a new use for a secret ingredient, or maybe a new tax benefit. So now you can tell your prospect what you just found out.

#3. Just continue to say, "I just found out ..." Nobody will notice. No one really cares about our lives, because they are focused on their own. Even if you talked to them yesterday, most people have forgotten or weren't listening anyway. In 40+ years of network marketing, no one has ever questioned me when I said, "I just found out ..."

I guess sometimes we just feel that we are an important element in other people's lives, but the reality is, they are totally focused on themselves and their problems, not us.

Party Time!

Let's say that I am your brand-new distributor, unskilled, no trained words, just beginning to learn how to prospect.

I go to a party and what happens when I want to approach a stranger? I hesitate because my words might bring me rejection. I look at the people at the party and think:

"Mm-hmm, I wonder if they'd be good? No, they might give me a rejection if I talked with them. I just don't know what to say to that person. That couple looks too important to want to do my business. Over there, he looks busy and probably wouldn't want to talk to me. That man looks mean."

And I leave the party with no prospects.

But you have Ice Breaker skills and you attended the same party. You talked to the very same 20 people that I only looked at. And you leave the party with five or six appointments for presentations the next day.

What was the difference? It's obvious now. You used "trained words" to get prospects to beg you for a presentation, rejection-free. The party was fun for you, and a self-image-crushing experience for me.

Remember, the exact same prospects, but two different results.

Don't Try This! It Is Only An Example.

Prospecting is not about finding the right person. Prospecting is all about knowing exactly what to say and do. We create our results.

If you don't believe this, do this experiment in your mind.

Imagine that you walk outside and see a stranger on the street. Walk up to that stranger and give that stranger $100 in cash.

Well, will that stranger react? Of course!

Maybe the stranger would give you a big hug, or shout that he won the lottery, or maybe ask you, "Do you have more cash to give me?"

Anyway, there would be a reaction by that stranger.

Now, imagine that you walk outside and see the exact same stranger on the street. This time, walk up to that stranger and give him a big punch in the nose!

Will that stranger react? Of course!

The stranger might punch you back, or maybe say, "Oh, that was rude."

Again, there would be a different reaction and a different behavior by that stranger.

Now, here is the big question.

"Did the behavior of that stranger have anything to do with the stranger? Or did the behavior of the stranger have everything to do with what you said or did?"

That explains prospecting. Most of the time, it is not about the prospect. Remember, prospects are pre-sold. They are simply reacting to how we approached them, if we built rapport, and if our Ice Breaker was interesting.

If we think about it, this is excellent news. That means that prospecting is within our control and we don't have to be lucky to succeed.

So let's rethink our Ice Breakers and the **reactions** they cause. Maybe we can also ask ourselves another question:

"Did the Ice Breaker I chose turn my prospect into a good prospect, looking for reasons to join? Or did it turn my prospect into a bad prospect, looking for reasons to run away?"

Formula #2.

I love the words, "Would it be okay if ..."

Humans are run by programs in their subconscious minds. One of the programs in our minds says this:

If anyone, anywhere, at any time, ever says the words "Would it be okay if ..." - the answer is YES!!!

That's right. Our minds make the "Yes" decision before we even hear the rest of the sentence. Weird. But it is just how we work. As long as the request is reasonable, the answer is almost always, "Yes."

Lots of programs are affected by these five words, but that's not important now. What is important is that it works.

Don't believe me? Have children.

Children are small people with no power and no money. Yet, they get anything they want. They know the power of certain word sequences. They learn this through trial and error, although sometimes I think they have a private network with other kids and share their secrets.

Has your daughter ever said this to you?

"Mom, Dad, would it be okay if I did my homework on Saturday instead?"

"Mom, Dad, would it be okay if I stayed at Heather's house tonight?"

"Mom, Dad, would it be okay if Cindy came with us to the mall?"

Where do you think I learned my collection of magic words? From my daughter, of course. She is a professional, and of course, consistently got almost anything she wanted.

There is a lot of power in the five words "Would it be okay if ..." - so let's use them to get our prospects to say "Yes" immediately. Once our prospect says "Yes," it is easy to schedule a presentation. What a great, rejection-free way to "break the ice" and get our business into our social conversations.

Here is Formula #2:

"Would it be okay if" + benefit = Great Ice Breaker

Ready for some examples? Let's talk about our business opportunity first:

* Would it be okay if you never had to show up to work again?

* Would it be okay if you had two paychecks instead of one?

* Would it be okay if you had five-day weekends instead of two-day weekends?

* Would it be okay if you earned more money?

* Would it be okay if you could sell your alarm clock to your neighbor?

* Would it be okay if you could wake up at the crack of noon?

* Would it be okay if you could fire the boss?

* Would it be okay if you never had to work overtime again?

* Would it be okay if you never had to work evenings again?

* Would it be okay if you could work from your home instead of commuting?

* Would it be okay if you could pick your own hours for work?

* Would it be okay if you could stay home with your children?

* Would it be okay if you could retire your husband from work?

* Would it be okay if you had an extra paycheck that would pay for your children's private school?

* Would it be okay if you could earn gangster money by helping people?

* Would it be okay if you could retire when you graduate from college?

It is easy to get prospects to say, "Yes. Tell me more." The hardest part of your business is finished. The prospect is now eager to talk to you.

But again you might be thinking, "Hey, wait a minute, these Formula #2 Ice Breakers are all about the opportunity. I want to talk about my product and services."

Okay, let's do some random products and service examples again. We are going to say, "Would it be okay if ..." and then add the following benefits. Ready?

For nutrition:

* Would it be okay if you had more stamina than your competitors?

* Would it be okay if you could help take care of your arthritis naturally?

* Would it be okay if you could get a good night's sleep every night by just drinking this juice every day?

* Would it be okay if you keep your parents healthier longer?

* Would it be okay if you felt great all day long with these magic pills?

* Would it be okay if you could slow down the aging process in your body?

* Would it be okay if you tried natural foods to help with your allergies?

* Would it be okay if you could sneak more nutrition into your children?

For skin care:

* Would it be okay if you never had to worry about acne again?

* Would it be okay if you could reduce fine lines and wrinkles in just seven minutes?

* Would it be okay if your skin could breathe all day long?

* Would it be okay if you could protect your skin from the sun without that oily feeling?

* Would it be okay if you looked younger than your daughter?

* Would it be okay if your skin got healthier while you sleep?

For diet products:

* Would it be okay if people stopped calling you, "Fat Harry?"

* Would it be okay if you burned body fat 24 hours a day?

* Would it be okay if you could lose weight and still eat your favorite foods?

* Would it be okay if you could lose weight by snacking on these bars between meals?

* Would it be okay if you could lose 15 pounds before the wedding?

* Would it be okay if you could lose 20 pounds before the class reunion?

* Would it be okay if you ate chocolate and still lost weight?

For utilities:

* Would it be okay if your electric bill was lower?

* Would it be okay if you paid less for your gas and electric?

* Would it be okay if you got rebates from your utility bill?

* Would it be okay if you took the discount instead of paying full retail?

* Would it be okay if your utility bill was easier to read?

For jewelry:

* Would it be okay if you could accessorize inexpensively?

* Would it be okay if your jewelry accented your best features?

* Would it be okay if your jewelry matched your wardrobe?

* Would it be okay if your jewelry was unique and different?

* Would it be okay if your jewelry got people to say, "WOW"?

For travel:

* Would it be okay if you had more holidays?

* Would it be okay if you could travel first-class?

* Would it be okay if you could travel to the places you dream about?

* Would it be okay if your holidays made you feel 100% relaxed?

* Would it be okay if your holidays were also awesome experiences?

* Would it be okay if your family reunions were on a cruise ship?

For natural cleaning products:

* Would it be okay if you helped the environment?

* Would it be okay if your laundry detergent was bio-degradable?

* Would it be okay if all your cleaners were natural and safe?

For financial services:

* Would it be okay if your bills got paid off faster?

* Would it be okay if your payments were less?

* Would it be okay if your insurance was affordable?

* Would it be okay if you could save for the future with one little change?

* Would it be okay if you paid less in taxes?

So, would it be okay if you tried some of these examples with the prospects you meet?

Formula #3.
(The Best Prospects)

Ask yourself this question, "Are the people around me generally positive, or generally negative?"

Most people admit that the people in their environment are generally negative. Very few of us are lucky enough to live in a totally positive, upbeat social circle.

Let's face it. Most people are negative. Why?

Because they have been beaten down by society, depressed from their daily grind, had their dreams crushed by their dream-sucking vampire bosses, are stressed by commuting in traffic, and ... well, life has problems.

And this is great!

The purpose of business is to solve people's problems. If people didn't have problems, there would be no reason for businesses to exist.

If no one got hungry, you certainly wouldn't want to own a restaurant.

If everyone was healthy forever, you wouldn't want to be a vitamin salesman.

If people never had to sleep, you would go broke owning that hotel.

You want people to have problems!

One summer I offered to do a workshop in the Ukraine on the Black Sea. Some leaders picked me up at the airport, and instantly started to tell me about all the problems in their business. Their conversation was something like this:

"Nobody in the Ukraine has any money. They can't afford a distributor kit. Our health products are too expensive. Our skin care products are too expensive. No one can buy products from us. The economy is terrible. Everything is so expensive. It is hard to live here now. And … we want you to fix all those problems for 500 distributors at tomorrow's workshop!"

The next day I explained to the 500 distributors that if people didn't have problems, they wouldn't have a business. So I asked them:

"Do Ukrainians want to live longer?"

"Do Ukrainians want their children to be healthy?"

"Do Ukrainians get wrinkles?"

"Is the Ukrainian winter hard on women's skin?"

"Is it hard to live on one salary in the Ukraine?"

"Do people in the Ukraine want more money?"

"Do Ukrainians want an opportunity to have a better life?"

And wow, the response from the group was great. They were glad to live in a country with the most problems! The distributors were hoping for even more problems in their lives.

Remember, if someone has a problem, they are a prospect. Stay away from all those positive people, they aren't prospects! (Just kidding.)

But listen to your downline talk.

"Oh, I don't have any prospects. Everyone I know is just so negative!"

Well, if they say that, you know that you haven't done a good job of training. They just don't **yet** understand that problems are our friends. We love negative people.

Negative people are the best prospects. You should go out of your way to locate negative people.

What I like most is that negative people:

1. Have a problem.

2. Know they have a problem. (Some people have a problem but don't know it. At least negative people know they have their problem because they are complaining about it.)

3. Have the option to use our solution to fix their problem, or to continue whining about the problem because it makes them feel happy to be so unhappy.

So let's make this work for us.

This Ice Breaker requires that you find large groups of negative people. (In Texas, we call these people family and friends.)

Next, you are going to listen to them whine, moan and complain. When they finally take a breath, you're going to say these exact words:

"Would you like to do something about it?"

Let's review. The prospect:

1. Has a problem

2. Knows he has a problem.

3. You have given him a choice, to fix the problem or not.

You're done!

What are the two possible answers?

"Yes" or "No."

If they say, "Yes, I'd like to do something about it," ka-ching! You are done. Take the money for their product order, fill out the application, whatever you need to do.

The prospect has made a decision to fix his problem.

I love this. In a room of 100 people, I can quickly locate the 20 or 30 people who want to fix their problems. Just a simple question: "Do you want to do something about it?" Everything else is easy.

Now, they could say, "No, I don't want to do something about it." Then I simply say, "And what else bothers you?" The prospect will continue with more negative stuff in his life, but I'll quietly slip away at the first opportunity.

Think about this. If the prospect says "No," and I ask about his other problems, at no time have I mentioned that I have a product or opportunity. I am just making conversation.

There is **zero** chance of rejection!

You might be wondering why prospects say, "No, I don't want to do something about it."

I have this theory. The reason prospects choose to tell you, "No" is because they mean "No." That's why they choose the word, "No."

"No" does not mean, "Please harass me for 52 more weeks."

"No" does not mean, "Please use neuro-linguistic programming kung-fu on me."

"No" means "No." Leave 'em alone. That way you still have family and friends. You won't be banned from weddings and funerals. You only want to deal with people who want to do something about their problem.

The challenge is that people will not tell you, "No." They are afraid you are going to argue with them, or they just don't want to hurt your feelings. They want to be polite and don't want to embarrass you. So if they want to tell you "No," but still want you to save face, they make up an imaginary excuse why they don't want your possible solution. They tell you "No," in **secret code**.

New distributors don't understand this. They think they have to argue with the imaginary objection. But once a new distributor understands that the prospect is really saying "No," then the new distributor can leave the prospect alone and get on with his life.

Let me give you an example of secret code.

I invite you to my house for dinner. You come over to my house and notice that my house is painted bright purple, even the windows. I say to you, "So how do you like the house?"

You are thinking, "Well, he hasn't fed me yet. I want to be polite."

So you reply, "It is interesting. It is colorful. It is unique."

That is secret code for, "Aaarrrgggghhh. It is terrible. I feel sick just looking at your purple house."

If you can't recognize when your prospects tell you "No" in secret code, you are going to waste so much time. You are going to irritate so many people. You won't have time to find all the good prospects who want to fix their problems.

How does this secret code sound in real life?

Example #1: You go home tonight. Your aunt is waiting for you. She says,

"My ankles hurt. My knees hurt. My hips hurt. My back hurts. My shoulders hurt. My neck hurts. I have migraine headaches. I have acid reflux, and that's a disease now, you know. I have five known diseases. Four unknown diseases. Three diseases they haven't even discovered yet."

And when your aunt finally takes a breath, you say, "Would you like to do something about it?"

If she says, "Yes," ka-ching! You are done. Take her money. Get her some products.

What's the other possible answer? "No."

But, your aunt will never tell you, "No." She'll tell you "No" in secret code. Let's see if you can recognize the secret code from your aunt's answer.

You say to your aunt, "Would you like to do something about it?"

And she says, "Oh, I'm under doctor's care."

That means "No."

Or if she says, "Well, the children visit me more when I pretend to be sick."

That means "No."

Or if she says, "Well, if I got better I wouldn't have anything to talk about then, would I?"

That means "No."

Or if she says, "Well, my mother died young. My grandmother died young. I want to die young just like them."

That means "No."

Or if she says, "Well, nothing works on me because I'm so special."

That means "No."

Or if she says, "Well, I can't swallow pills or liquids."

That means "No."

Now when your aunt says "No" in secret code, you will simply say,

"And what else bothers you?"

Listen to her complain about the potholes in the street that the city hasn't fixed, etc., grab your worthless brother-in-law, put him in front of you, and slowly slip away while your aunt continues to complain.

Whenever a prospect says, "No," the next thing you say is,

"And what else bothers you?"

No rejection. And in less than a minute you have determined this person isn't a prospect. They just enjoy complaining too much. How easy is that?

Let me give you some more examples. You go home tonight, your aunt is waiting for you, and your aunt says,

"Oh, my skin is so dry. I have dry skin flakes everywhere. When my dog jumps on the sofa, it looks like a snowstorm because the flakes fly everywhere. I have this oily spot right in the middle of my forehead. I have eczema breaking out on my neck. And I have wrinkles so deep I can store food in them!"

When she finally takes a breath, you are going to say, "Would you like to do something about it?"

If she says, "Yes," ka-ching! You are done. Sell her some skin care products.

What's the other possible answer?

"No."

But remember she will never tell you, "No." She will tell you that she is not interested in **secret code**.

Let's see if you can recognize the secret code this time.

Your aunt answers:

"Well, that oily spot in the middle of my forehead makes my hat slip on so much better. I am allergic to everything. My sister-in-law sells the only brand of skin care I can use. And when my dog jumps on the sofa, it reminds me of winter when I was a child."

What are you going to say?

"And what else bothers you?"

And your aunt will continue talking about the other problems in her life while you slip away as quickly as you can.

Need another example?

You go to work. While standing by the coffee machine, Joe says to you,

"My car broke down this morning, and I don't have the money to fix it. I have the MasterCard, Visa, and the American Express bills coming in. I haven't been able to pay my car insurance and the car payment is due. I'm two house payments behind. The boss won't give me a raise. I didn't have money to go on holiday last year."

And when Joe finally takes a breath, what are you going to say?

"Would you like to do something about it?"

If Joe says, "Yes," ka-ching! Invite Joe to a meeting, give him a CD, DVD, send Joe to your website, talk to him privately at lunch, or enroll him in your business. All of these options are available to you.

What's the other possible answer?

"No."

Let's see if you can recognize the secret code.

"Well, I'm only 44 years away from retirement, and I don't want to mess that up. And this sounds like a pyramid. Plus my father died broke, my grandfather died broke and I want to die broke just like them. Nothing good ever happens to me. I don't have any money. I don't know anybody. I only know three people and two of them hate me. And by the time I finish watching eight hours of television every evening, I just don't have time to do anything else."

Joe is telling us, "No." So what should we say?

"And what else bothers you?"

All you have to do is find people who whine, moan and complain, quickly check if they want to do something about their problems, and take the volunteers!

I bet you just can't wait to find some negative people. They are the best!

I will have to caution you about one thing.

If you keep asking people, "Would you like to do something about it?" - then after a while your relatives will notice the trend. They will stop complaining to you because they know what you will say next.

Hmmm, that's not so bad, is it?

Think of prospecting this way:

We don't want to irritate people. We just want to help those people who have a problem, and want to fix their problem.

You can use this Ice Breaker with almost any product.

Let me give you one more example.

I am overweight and anyone would have to be blind not to notice. So I say to you:

"Well, you know I've been trying to lose weight, but it's really, really hard to lose weight. I'm very big-boned. Plus I have a metabolism problem. I've been eating just donuts to lose weight because they have a hole in the middle, so you would think I'd lose weight. And I bought these exercise videos. My thumb has a blister on it from pressing fast forward, and I still haven't lost weight."

When I take a breath from my complaining, you say, "Would you like to do something about it?"

I reply, "Yes!"

How easy would it be to take my order for some diet products? Networking is easy when we know what to say.

But how would "No" sound in secret code for my dieting problems?

"Nothing works for me. I tried to exercise once, broke out in a sweat, must be allergic to that. I get hungry at night. I have to keep up my strength. It isn't fat, it is my stomach-bicep. My whole family is fat, etc."

Just remember these magic words:

"Would you like to do something about it?"

And if that is too strong for your tastes, you can cushion it a little by saying this:

"Have you ever considered doing something about it?"

Yes, the question you ask is important, but the more important skill is listening to the answer to make sure they are not trying to tell you "No" in secret code.

I love negative people!

Formula #4.
(Creating The Prospect)

You might be thinking,

"I can't possibly use Ice Breaker #3. Everyone I know is so positive. I never meet negative people!

"When I stand by the coffee machine at work, my co-workers are saying,

"Oh my goodness, look at my paycheck. They have overpaid me again! There's never any traffic when I drive to work. My children are perfect. My sports team always wins. My favorite brand of beer is always on sale.

"Life is wonderful where I live. No one ever has a problem or a negative thought."

Well, if all of your prospects are positive, you certainly couldn't use Ice Breaker #3.

For positive people, you will have to learn Ice Breaker #4:

How to induce negativity!

You can induce negativity instantly on demand with one simple sentence.

Simply say:

"What are your two biggest _____
problems?"

You can't help someone if they don't have problems! So let's see how this works.

You come home after work and your uncle is there, drinking your beer. He is so happy. He says:

"Ahhh, my favorite sports team won today. My favorite brand of beer is on sale. My car's running better than ever before. I get such good fuel mileage now, every morning I have to drain the extra gas out of my car. I feel great!"

Somewhere in the conversation with your uncle you might say, "So what are your two biggest **career** problems?"

Your uncle replies, "Career? I don't have a career. The boss hates my guts. I had to work overtime three days last week, missed my daughter's violin concert while doing these stupid reports that nobody ever reads. And the person next to me clips their toenails at work. I hate that."

When your uncle finally takes a breath, what are you going to say?

"Would you like to do something about it?"

And if your uncle says, "Yes," ka-ching!

You know what to do next from Ice Breaker #3.

Or, on the way home from work, you stop for a cup of coffee, and the waitress says, "Ahh, _Desperate Housewives_ ended just the way I wanted. It was fantastic. And they just renewed my driver's license with a decent picture this time.

Tomorrow is the big 50% off shopping day. Can't wait. Beautiful day again today."

You say to the waitress, "So what are your two biggest problems with waitressing at night?

And she replies, "Well, first of all I missed *Desperate Housewives* when it aired. I got to watch the reruns after all my friends knew how it ended. With working nights, I don't see my kids when they come home from school. And you know, working nights, I have to serve loud drunks and cheap people who won't leave a tip!"

You say, "Would you like to do something about it?"

And if she says, "Yes," ka-ching!

You know what to do next from Ice Breaker #3.

Or, you come home from work and your aunt is waiting for you. Your aunt says, "The birthday party I attended today was wonderful. The dresses were so cute. The balloons were the perfect color."

You say, "So Auntie, what are your two biggest skin care problems?"

She replies, "Oh I have eczema so bad, when I scratch it, it bleeds and it starting to tie-dye my clothes. I don't want to tie-dye my clothes, because it doesn't look fashionable like it did back in the '70s. When I scratch, those dry flakes from my skin go everywhere, and now my dog is allergic to my skin flakes. And my wrinkles, my goodness. They are getting so deep, I can't even see the bottom of them!"

You say, "Auntie, would you like to do something about it?"

And if she says, "Yes," ka-ching!

You know what to do next from Ice Breaker #3.

Pretty simple. Just make people think about their problems, and give them a chance to say they want to do something about their problems. Remember, we are in the problem-fixing business.

I should add a disclaimer here for distributors who sell health products.

Be careful if you ask, "What are your two biggest _____ problems?"

This is one question that should only be asked by a professional in our business. Why? Yes, this is a powerful question, but if you are not careful, it could take up a lot of your time.

Let's say you are at a party, and you ask someone, "Mary, what are your two biggest health problems?"

Be careful. She might say:

"Have a seat, volume one!"

Six hours later she is still recounting every drug and procedure! If you want to get back the time you need in your life, what are you going to say?

"Mary, would you like to do something about it?" or "Mary, have you ever considered doing something about it?"

On the plus side, you have made a friend for life. You are probably the first person who has asked her to describe all of her suffering. Even her closest relatives would not listen to her, but you did. You actually created super-strong rapport, so this little question could give you unlimited nutrition sales.

Here are some quick examples of questions:

* What are your two biggest problems working at fast food restaurants at night?

* What are the two biggest problems with commuting to work?

* What are the two biggest problems working at hotels?

* What are your two biggest problems with shift work?

* What are your two biggest cleaning problems?

* What are your two biggest problems with dieting?

* What are your two biggest problems … ?

Well, you get the idea.

So don't worry about running across an occasional positive person. It happens. Just use Ice Breaker #4 to induce negativity instantly. Then solve his or her problem.

Formula #5.

Most countries have informal laws about what you say at a party when meeting someone new. People are required to ask these three questions in the proper order.

Question #1: "What is your name?"

Question #2: "Where do you live?"

Question #3: "What do you do for a living?"

Sound familiar? (No, it is not a real law.)

So, you are at a party. Someone asks you, "What do you do for a living?"

Do you think your answer has the power to turn that person into a good prospect looking for reasons to join, or a bad prospect looking for reasons not to join?

Of course. So we must carefully select our answer and use the proper words so that this prospect will **ask** us for a presentation.

Now, when I first got started, how many skills did I have? None. Introverted nerds, engineering students, quiet accountants, scientists, shy people ... that was my group of friends. We didn't even know that social and communication skills existed.

When people asked me, "What do you do for a living?" … I panicked. No one had taught me specific words to use. My responses were generally verbal diarrhea that turned ordinary people into bad prospects.

Some examples of my disastrous answers?

* "I am in the global search for entrepreneurial talent, for time freedom and financial freedom, whereby they can enhance their efforts through multiple streams of residual income thereby …" Arrrgghhh. That was bad.

* "I am with the Wonderful Company from the wonderful city with the wonderful founder who walks on water when it is frozen, with the wonderful patented product picked underneath rocks in China at midnight by elves …" You already know how awful that one is.

* "I am chief executive officer and executive recruiter with Mysterious Name Corporation …"

These kinds of answers aren't what people want to hear at parties. They just want a simple explanation of what we do. They want us to say something like, "Carpenter. Pizza maker. Bank vice-president. Farmer. Circus performer." Then they will say, "Uh, yeah." They really aren't listening anyway and are just being polite.

After continuous disasters, I thought, "How do I explain this? Network marketing is different than a job, isn't it? Prospects don't want the entire presentation."

Think about it. When prospects say, "What do you do for a living?" you don't want to say, "Wait, let me go out to the car and get my PowerPoint, DVD, flip chart and easel." That might be a bit much right?

Prospects just want to know **generally** what you do. But how do you explain something a bit more complicated such as network marketing? Do you say,

"Well, in my business you buy my company's products at wholesale, then sell those products at retail. The differential is the retail profit, which is the gross profit, not the net profit, depending on your taxable situation and you have generations of people who talk to other people, and it grows slowly in the beginning, but later you can take trips if your BV and PV is enough to qualify …"

Where do you start? Where do you end?

So let's get a good explanation now and stop losing all that bonus money because we never could get people interested.

Two more examples of disasters.

When I started, all of my Ice Breaker formulas were a disaster. You really want to avoid the following two formulas.

First, people would ask me what I did for a living. I didn't know what to say, so I said **nothing**. Believe me, that was not effective. People just looked at me like I was an idiot who didn't even know what I did for a living!

Second, I knew I would have to say something, so when more people asked me, "What do you do for a living?" - to avoid embarrassment, I would simply change the subject. I would say, "Well, what I do is … hey look! There's Superman!" That did change the subject, and it did stop my embarrassment temporarily, but still produced no effective results.

One day I finally noticed that people are **reactive**. Remember how the stranger reacted to you when you gave him $100? And how the stranger had a different reaction when you punched him in the nose?

The principle is this.

"People **react to you**, and **you** can control **you**."

Simply change what you say and do, and people will react differently.

A better solution.

People are going to ask you what you do for a living. Remember, the words you choose in your answer will either:

1. Turn them into good prospects, looking for reasons to join. Make them ask you for more information, begging you for a presentation.

Or, …

2. Turn them into bad prospects that will quickly change the topic and say, "Oh, and how is the weather where you live?" And then, they'll quickly make an excuse to talk to someone else.

Think about it. People **have** to react. So how would you like them to react to what you say?

I bet you would want this reaction. After you tell the prospects what you do for a living, their reaction would be to tell you,

"Oh really? How does that work?"

You have turned these prospects into good prospects, looking for reasons to join. They are asking you for more information, begging you for a presentation.

Now, if you know the exact reaction you want from people, wouldn't it be easy to create some words to get that reaction?

The words I love to hear from prospects are:

"Oh really? How does that work?"

If your trained answer to the question, "What do you do for a living?" got the response: "Oh really? How does that work?" - wouldn't it be easy to continue from there? Your prospect is excited about what you said and is **asking** for a presentation.

Here is Formula #5.

If you ask me, "What I do for a living?" - I will use Formula #5 which is:

"I show people how to _____ + solve a problem."

Now, this gets easy. You are going to recognize these problems. Ready?

* I show people how to fire their boss.

* I show people how to get an extra paycheck.

* I show people how to get stop commuting and work at home.

* I show people how to choose their own hours to work.

Do you see how we are solving problems? Prospects want to fire their boss, get an extra paycheck to pay bills, stop spending long hours commuting and choose their own working hours. Prospects will love you when you solve their problems and they will react and respond with:

"Oh really? How does that work?"

This is way too easy, isn't it?

Just solve problems. Put the problem or put a benefit that solves a problem after the words, "I show people how to ..."

Want some more examples?

For opportunity:

* I show people how to retire ten years early at full pay.

* I show people how to work only three weeks a month but get paid for four weeks.

* I show people how to be in their own business so they get more tax benefits.

* I show people how to start their own part-time business to create wealth quickly.

* I show people how to never have to show up to work again.

* I show people how to take a six-month holiday, three times a year. (Well, it would at least get their attention.)

* I show people how to wake up in the morning when they are tired of sleeping.

* I show people how to make more money than their boss.

* I show teachers how to earn money without the stress of teaching.

* I show grandmothers how to make their life interesting and get paid for it.

* I show policemen how to have a new career so their spouses won't worry about them every day.

* I show high school graduates how to buy a college instead of attending a college. (Okay, maybe a bit of exaggeration here, but it makes this formula easy to remember.)

For nutrition:

* I show people how to wake up before the alarm clock, totally energized.

* I show people how to sleep like a baby every night.

* I show people how to laugh at arthritis and joint pain by changing what they drink in the morning.

* I show grandmothers how to have the smartest grandchildren in their school.

* I show people how to laugh at hay fever season again.

* I show people how to have more energy - naturally.

For skin care:

* I show mothers how to look younger than their daughters.

* I show people how to reduce the bags under their eyes naturally.

* I show people how to remove stretch marks in 21 days.

* I show people how to make their skin feel so soft and young, that they can't stop touching it.

* I show people how to make their skin so fresh and clean that they won't need makeup.

For diet products:

* I show people how to fit into their "skinny jeans" easily.

* I show people how to lose weight one time and keep it off forever.

* I show people how to drink off their body weight with a special chocolate shake.

* I show people how to look fit with a special 30-day body makeover.

* I show people how to lose weight even if they cheat.

For travel:

* I show people how to travel at travel agent prices.

* I show people how to stop taking holidays at their mother-in-law's house.

* I show people how to save money when staying at luxury hotels.

* I show people how to have vacations that other people can only talk about.

* I show people how to find secret deals on great vacations.

For natural cleaning products:

* I show mothers how to get rid of their toxic cleaners and replace them naturally.

* I show people how to use child-safe detergents when cleaning.

* I show people how to save our environment by switching to biodegradable household products.

For financial services:

* I show people how to save for their retirement without ruining their monthly budget.

* I show people how to get out of debt fast, and have sparkling good credit.

* I show people how to create a savings account from their current monthly expenses.

* I show people how to save money on their taxes so they can enjoy more of life instead of less.

Yes, it is incredibly easy to get our prospects to say:

"Oh really? How does that work?"

Of course not everyone will answer this way. Some people aren't listening, or may not be interested in what you do for a living. These non-prospects will simply answer: "And how's the weather where you live?"

That is an easy way for them to exit from this part of the conversation, and this exit is rejection-free to you also. No harm done. No rejection.

But ... but ... but ...

You might be thinking, "Oh, this is awesome. Somebody asks me what I do for a living, I use Ice Breaker Formula #5, but wait. I only have **one** person a month ask me what I do for a living, and I could starve waiting for that to happen every month!"

That's a good concern. However, picture this.

There are 1,000 people outside your front door right now, all lined up in single file. Each person has a little card that instructs them to ask you what you do for a living, and each person comes up to you, one at a time, and says,

"What do you do for a living?"

If you gave each person your best answer using Ice Breaker Formula #5, don't you think you would have all the volunteers you would ever need to sponsor for your entire career? It would be easy!

You could be picky. Some of the 1,000 people are not going to be interested. Some are going to be interested. Just take the easy ones. For example, you could say to prospect #671, "I don't really like the way you look. Next." ☺

No one is forcing you to take or convince anyone. You simply accept the easy volunteers who respond favorably to your answer when you are asked what you do for a living.

Of course, that's if life was perfect. But life is not perfect, and you don't have 1,000 people outside your front door. But, what if three or four people every day came up to you and asked you what you did for a living? How many people would that be in a year? Over 1,000 people. Hmmmm.

Now, think about this. If you wanted three or four people every day to come up to you and ask you what you do for a living, what would you have to do to make that happen?

All you have to do is ask three or four people what **they** do for a living first.

These people will spend about 10 minutes talking about their long, boring non-network-marketing lives. And when they're done, they're probably going to say, "And by the way, what do you do for a living?"

And you know exactly how to answer that question to create a prospect, begging you for a presentation.

So if you want 1,000 people to ask you, "What do you do for a living?" — all you have to do is ask three or four people each day, "What do you do for a living?"

In one year, you could have all the personally-sponsored people you need just with this one simple technique.

Extremely Shy Distributors Can Do This.

Let's say that I am an extremely shy distributor in your group. I want to be successful, meet strangers and build a group, but I am afraid to talk to people.

That's not going to work well, is it?

But as my sponsor, you can help me become a powerful leader with a huge group by using this simple conversation.

Big Al: "Oh, I want to be successful, but I am too shy to talk to people about my business. What should I do?"

You: "Well Big Al, the first thing I want you to do is to **not** tell anyone about your business. Just keep it top secret. Can you do that?"

Big Al: "Uh, yes. I certainly could do that."

You: "Next, I don't want you to ever say anything about our products or services. Don't tell anyone. Can you do that?"

Big Al: "Uh, yes. I certainly could do that. Hey, I think this is a lot more comfortable for me. By the way, what do you want me to do?"

You: "All I want you to do is help me create World Peace. That's it. Now, you have heard the saying, 'Think globally, but work locally.'"

Big Al: "Yes, I have heard that. But creating World Peace is a big job, isn't it? I would like to help, even locally. So what would you like me to do locally?"

You: "The easiest way to create World Peace is to help three or four people feel good about themselves every day. Could you do that?"

Big Al: "Happy to do that. But how do I help three or four people a day feel good about themselves?"

You: "Simple. Just get them to talk about themselves. People love to talk about themselves."

Big Al: "Sounds great, but how do I get people to talk about themselves?"

You: "Easy. Just ask them a question."

Big Al: "Uh, but what question could I ask them?"

You: "How about asking them what they do for a living? That's an easy question for them to answer, and they love talking about themselves."

Big Al: "Okay, got it. I just ask three or four people every day what they do for a living, they talk about themselves, and I help create World Peace. I can do that."

You: "Great. Oh, by the way. Sometimes when people finish talking about what they do for a living, they might ask you what you do for a living. You should answer them. It would be impolite for you to answer, 'Can't tell you. Top secret.' So if someone asks you what you do for a living, simply say, 'I show people how to fire their boss.' And that's it.

Big Al: "Okay, I hope they don't ask me. I'm shy. But if they do, I will answer, 'I show people how to fire their boss.'

You: "Oh, by the way, sometimes when you answer, 'I show people how to fire their boss.' — the other person might ask you, 'Oh really? How does that work?' If they ask you that, don't panic. Just tell them that I can answer that question for you, and that I will call them."

Big Al: "Whew. Thanks. I'll refer anyone to you that asks that question. Maybe later on I can learn to answer it myself."

Do you see a plan where even the shyest person in the world can build a business? Simply by asking three or four people a day, "What do you do for a living?" — almost anyone can locate enough volunteers to build a huge and successful business.

Shy people are great. They are just shy, not lazy. They too want to build a business.

Formula #6.

There is a second way to answer the question, "What do you do for a living?" It is a bit more complicated, but some distributors like it better. Why?

Because prospects are lazy. They don't want to think. And this formula does all the thinking for them. You see, when you tell a prospect what you do for a living, the prospect has to think, "Would this solve a problem that I have?"

So instead of having the prospect figure this out, let's do the hard work for the prospect. Here is the formula:

1. "Well, you know how ... (problem)"

2. "Well, what I do is ... (solution)"

Now, if you have read my book, "How To Get Instant Trust, Belief, Influence and Rapport! 13 Ways To Create Open Minds By Talking to the Subconscious Mind," you already know how powerful the phrase "Well, you know how ..." is to prospects. Prospects will immediately accept what you say as true. That's a big step. Your prospect won't question that the problem you describe is not a real problem for many people.

Then, when you explain what you do for a living, you will provide a solution to that problem. It is easier to demonstrate than to actually explain.

Let's say someone asked you, "What do you do for a living?"

You could reply:

"Well, you know how we all get lots of bills in the mail every month? **Well, what I do is** show people how to get an extra paycheck in their mailbox to pay all those bills."

What is your prospect thinking? He might be thinking, "Yeah, I get a mortgage payment, a tax bill, a MasterCard bill, a car loan payment, an insurance payment ... wow, I get a lot of bills. And yes, it would be great to get an extra paycheck in the mailbox to pay all those bills. I've got to know more!"

Again, the prospect is asking us for presentation. Life is good.

Here are more examples of what your answer could be if someone asked you, "What do you do for a living?"

For opportunity:

* Well, you know how we all hate our jobs? Well, I show people how to fire their boss.

* Well, you know how most jobs don't pay enough? Well, I show people how to get a second paycheck to make life a lot easier.

* Well, you know how we hate commuting in traffic and wasting all that time away from our family? Well, I show people how to work out of their homes.

* Well, you know how things are so expensive now? Well, I show people how to have more money with a fun part-time business.

* Well, you know how it is hard to get by on even two paychecks now? Well, I show people how to start their own part-time business, so they can earn all the money they need.

* Well, you know how some people have a problem with having too much month and too little money? Well, I show people how to get an extra paycheck in their mailbox every month to take care of that problem.

* Well, you know how weekends are too short? Well, I show people how to have a five-day weekend every week.

* Well, you know how there is never any money left over for savings? Well, I show families how to have a part-time business that fills their savings account quickly.

For nutrition:

* Well, you know how growing old really hurts? Well, I show people how to stop that aging process and feel younger in just seven days.

* Well, you know how grandchildren can quickly become little house-wreckers? Well, I show grandmothers how to have more energy than their grandchildren.

* Well, you know how we want to protect our children from all the germs at school? Well, I show mothers how to protect them with a simple juice drink every morning.

* Well, you know how we want our children healthy and hate taking off work to take them to the doctor? Well, I show mothers how to have the healthiest children in their neighborhood.

* Well, you know how some people always have to monitor their blood sugar levels? Well, I show people how to lower their blood sugar levels without drugs and medication.

* Well, you know how we all feel tired after a long day at work? Well, I show people how to have three more hours of energy every evening.

* Well, you know how a lot of people feel like taking a nap at about 2:00pm in the afternoon after they had a big lunch? And, when they come home from work, they flop into an easy chair, grab the remote control and hope somebody brings them food before they fall asleep? Well, I show people how to take special vitamins in the morning so that they have energy all day long.

For skin care:

* Well, you know how wrinkles give us "character?" Well, I show women how to keep wrinkles away for an extra ten years.

* Well, you know how we hate putting steroid creams on our children's eczema? Well, I show moms how to use natural products to help their children have clear skin.

* Well, you know how we hate wrinkling more while we sleep? Well, I show women how to use a special night cream so that their skin gets younger while they sleep.

* Well, you know how we all wish our skin was softer? Well, I show women how to make their skin softer in three days with a magic lotion.

* Well, you know how we all wish we could make our skin younger and younger? Well, I show women how to make their skin younger every night, and after just a few weeks, they won't even be able to order alcohol at a restaurant!

For diet products:

* Well, you know how we just don't have time to exercise? Well, I show people how to stay fit just by changing what they have for breakfast.

* Well, you know how hard it is to lose weight, even if we only eat the outside of our donuts? Well, I show people how to lose weight even if they also eat the donut hole!

* Well, you know how it is hard to eat right because we are so busy? Well, I show people how to turn their bodies into fat-burning machines.

* Well, you know how hard it is to lose weight, especially when we are big-boned, or have a thyroid or metabolism problem? Well, I show people how to lose weight by resetting their inner metabolism.

* Well, you know how we all like to eat pizza and desserts. Well, I show people how to use some magic tablets so that those sugar and fat calories don't stick to their hips.

* Well, you know how exercise is painful? Well, I show people how to lose weight without all that hard exercise and pain.

* Well, you know how a lot of people are always starving themselves, exercising, eating funny foods and the weight keeps coming back? Well, I show people how to lose weight easily with our special protein drink.

* Well, you know how many of us are allergic to exercise because it makes us turn red and break out in a sweat? Well, I show people how to be trim and fit while laughing at their former personal trainer. (Okay, maybe I am going too far.)

For travel:

* Well, you know how we don't have time to travel because our job takes up all of our time? Well, I show people how to take great mini-vacations that fit into their schedule.

* Well, you know how we want great family memories? Well, I show families how to take dream vacations at a price they can afford.

* Well, you know how expensive travel can be? Well, I show people how to travel at wholesale rates.

* Well, you know how we end up taking affordable vacations by staying with our in-laws? Well, I show families how to take exciting vacations that still fit into their budgets.

* Well, you know how we all want travel bargains, but don't know where to find them? Well, I show people great travel bargains for the destinations they want.

For natural cleaning products:

* Well, you know how we all want to help the environment but we don't have time? Well, I show people how to make a big difference by simply changing out the toxic cleaners in their homes.

* Well, you know how we don't want poisonous chemicals and cleaners in our home when children live there 24 hours a day? Well, I help families use natural, safe cleaners in their homes.

* Well, you know how we want to use organic cleaners, but they don't clean as well as the harsher commercial laundry detergents? Well, I show people how to use a special natural, concentrated laundry detergent that cleans their clothes better and safer.

For financial services:

* Well, you know how it is almost impossible to save money now with the cost of living so high? Well, I show people how to use tax advantages to fund all their savings.

* Well, you know how insurance is so expensive, but we need it? Well, I show families how to get inexpensive insurance so that they still have money to enjoy life.

* Well, you know how hard it is to get out of debt? Well, I show people how to pay off their debts quickly so that they have more money to enjoy life.

* Well, you know how we are all going to die? Well, I show people how to manage their money so that they can

party and have a great time before they die. (Okay, am I going too far yet?)

Yes, a little exaggeration helps us remember. This is another great way to answer the question, "What do you do for a living?"

And Finally ...

Is it easy to get prospects to beg you for a presentation now?

Yes!

Just go back to that original party and see all the different Ice Breaker formulas we could use. The prospects at the party don't have a chance! If there were only 20 people at the party, we could easily have 8 or 10 people asking us for presentations. We could use:

1. I just found out.

2. Would it be okay if ...

3. Find negative people.

4. Find positive people and make them negative.

5. I show people how to ...

6. Well, you know how (problem).

Going to parties now would be fun instead of a fearful exercise in rejection. The difference?

Trained words. Knowing exactly what to say.

And that is why we need to give our new distributors a chance with trained words. New distributors don't know how to talk to people correctly yet. They are just starting. So keep them from using untrained, unskilled, verbal diarrhea words, and getting discouraged. Teach them professional Ice Breakers now.

You might be wondering, "Why do we need so many different Ice Breaker formulas?"

Well, if we only knew one formula, we would be limited. Let me give you an example.

Let's say that you only knew one way to break the ice. You knew how to say, "What do you do for a living?" And, you had a great answer. You would still miss opportunities.

One night after the opportunity meeting, you stop by a fast food restaurant and order a hamburger and French fries. You then say to the clerk, "What do you do for a living?"

Aaaarrrggghhh.

Yes, it is good to have multiple ways of breaking the ice. Asking your co-workers, "What do you do for a living?" might be awkward also.

There are hundreds of Ice Breakers we can use. This book should give you a good understanding of what an Ice Breaker can do.

If you've read, "How To Get Instant Trust, Belief, Influence and Rapport! 13 Ways To Create Open Minds By Talking To The Subconscious Mind," you probably learned a great Ice Breaker that starts with these four words:

"I am just curious …"

You will certainly observe and learn more Ice Breakers now that you are aware of how easy they can be.

Just one more thing:

Remember that all Ice Breakers work better when you use them.

Free!

Get 7 mini-reports of amazing, easy sentences that create new, hot prospects.

Discover how just a **few correct words** can change your network marketing results forever.

Get all seven <u>free</u> Big Al mini-reports, and the <u>free</u> weekly Big Al Report with more recruiting and prospecting tips.

Sign up today at:
http://www.BigAlReport.com

Want Big Al to speak in your area?

Request a Big Al training event:
http://www.BigAlSeminars.com

Tom "Big Al" Schreiter's books
are available at:
http://www.BigAlBooks.com

See a full line of Big Al products at:
http://www.FortuneNow.com

ABOUT THE AUTHOR

Tom "Big Al" Schreiter has 40+ years of experience in network marketing and MLM. As the author of the original "Big Al" training books in the late '70s, he has continued to speak in over 80 countries on using the exact words and phrases to get prospects to open up their minds and say "YES."

His passion is marketing ideas, marketing campaigns, and how to speak to the subconscious mind in simplified, practical ways. He is always looking for case studies of incredible marketing campaigns that give usable lessons.

As the author of numerous audio trainings, Tom is a favorite speaker at company conventions and regional events.

His blog, http://www.BigAlBlog.com , is a regular update of network marketing and MLM business-building ideas.

Anyone can subscribe to his free weekly tips at:

http://www.BigAlReport.com

23846638R00060

Made in the USA
Middletown, DE
04 September 2015